WORLD IN PERIL

CITIES

IN CRISIS

PAUL MASON

Raintree

www.raintreepublishers.co.uk
Visit our website to find out
more information about
Raintree books.

To order:
☎ Phone 0845 6044371
🖹 Fax +44 (0) 1865 312263
🖳 Email myorders@capstonepub.co.uk

Customers from outside the UK please telephone +44 1865 312262

©Raintree is an imprint of Capstone Global Library
Limited, a company incorporated in England and Wales having
its registered office at 7 Pilgrim Street, London, EC4V 6LB
- Registered company number: 6695582

"Raintree" is a registered trademark of Pearson Education
Limited, under licence to Capstone Global Library Limited

Text © Capstone Global Library Limited 2009
First published in hardback in 2009
Paperback edition first published in 2010

Edited by Louise Galpine and Rachel Howells
Designed by Richard Parker and Manhattan Design
Picture research by Hannah Taylor and Rebecca Sodergren
Production by Alison Parsons
Originated by Dot Gradations Ltd.
Printed in China by Leo Paper Products Ltd.

ISBN 978 0 431020 59 4 (hardback)
13 12 11 10 09
10 9 8 7 6 5 4 3 2 1

ISBN 978 0 431020 66 2 (paperback)
14 13 12 11 10
10 9 8 7 6 5 4 3 2 1

British Library Cataloguing in Publication Data
Mason, Paul
Cities in Crisis. – (World in peril)
577.5'6

A full catalogue record for this book is available from the
British Library.

Acknowledgements
We would like to thank the following for permission to
reproduce photographs: Alamy Images pp. **8** (Steve Allen
Travel Photography), **22** (Kathy deWitt), **26** (ICP); City of
Melbourne council p. **15**; Corbis pp. **10** (B.Mathur), **12** (Alan
Hindle); Getty Images pp. **6** (Angelo Cavalli), **17** (Guang Niu),
24 (Greg Pease); Panos pp. **7** (Crispin Hughes), **27** (David
Rose); Photolibrary pp. **4** (Phillip Hayson), **11** and **18** (JTB
Photo), **14** (F1 Online), **16** (Chad Ehlers), **20** (age fotostock),
25 (Hans Georg Eiben); Reuters pp. **9** (Eduardo Munoz), **13**
(Toby Melville), **19** (Vito Lee), **21** (Katrina Manson); Rex
Features p. **23** (Sipa Press).

Cover photograph of pollution over Shanghai, China,
reproduced with permission of Corbis (Bohemian Nomad
Picturemakers/ Kevin R. Morris).

We would like to thank Michael Mastrandrea for his invaluable
help in the preparation of this book.

Every effort has been made to contact copyright holders of
material reproduced in this book. Any omissions will be
rectified in subsequent printings if notice is given to the
publishers.

All the Internet addresses (URLs) given in this book were valid
at the time of going to press. However, due to the dynamic
nature of the Internet, some addresses may have changed, or
sites may have changed or ceased to exist since publication.
While the author and Publishers regret any inconvenience this
may cause readers, no responsibility for any such changes can
be accepted by either the author or the Publishers.

Contents

Some words are printed in bold, **like this**. You can find out what they mean by looking in the glossary.

What is the problem with cities?

This is Sydney, Australia, a city of over four million people. In 2007, for the first time ever, more people throughout the world lived in **urban** areas than in **rural** ones. The number of people who live in cities is growing all the time. So how can cities be in crisis?

The answer is that our cities were not designed to hold so many people. In many cities, there isn't enough space for everyone. As a result, it is hard for people to find somewhere to live. The roads are **congested** with all the traffic. The **sewers** and water supplies cannot cope. It is increasingly hard to get food to all of the world's city **dwellers**. We are running out of places to put the rubbish that our cities produce.

By 2050, the world's population is expected to grow to nine billion – three billion more than in 2000. All these people will need somewhere to live, and most of them will live in cities. If we cannot find ways to solve some of the problems in our cities, things will get even worse in the future.

What kind of city life would you prefer?

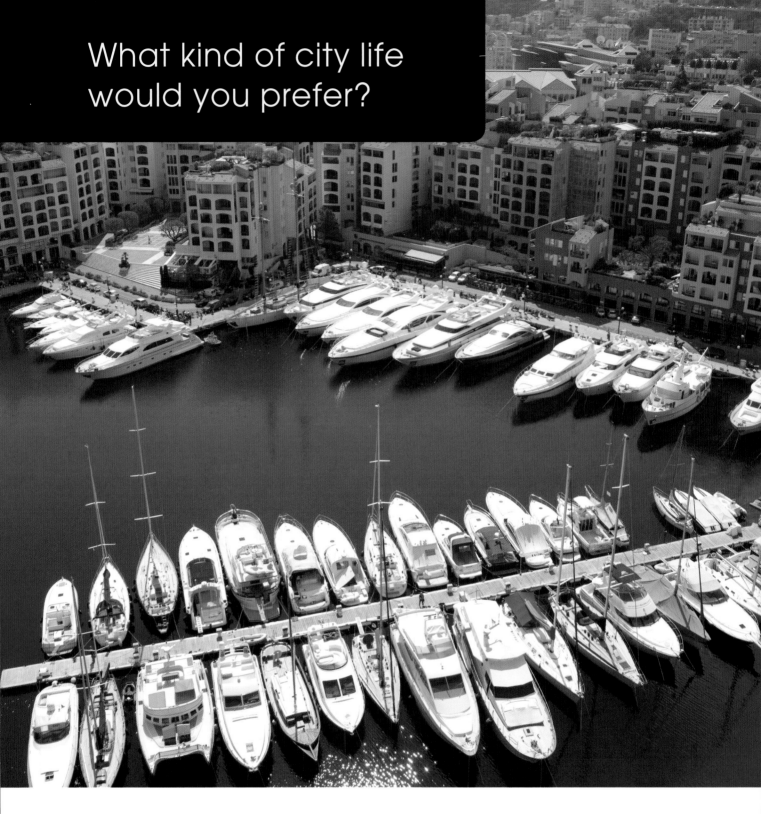

How would you like to live in a place such as Monte Carlo, perched on the edge of the Mediterranean Sea? The city has everything you could want: cinemas, restaurants, sports centres, good schools, and other **facilities**.

Even in Monte Carlo and cities like it, not everybody has a good life. Plenty of people find the cost of food and housing too high. They struggle to pay the bills each month.

These people live on the edge of Nairobi, in Kenya. Many of them came to the city dreaming of the kind of life shown on page 6. However, jobs and houses were very hard to find.

These homes have been built **illegally**, on land that nobody else wanted. Often the walls are made of thin wood, metal, or even cardboard. There are no toilets, and probably no power in many of the houses.

Do cities always get enough food?

How far do you think these vegetables and fruits travelled to reach this market in Rajasthan, India? Today, almost all of the food that city **dwellers** eat is grown somewhere else, then brought to the city to be sold.

Every day, thousands of lorries, trains, planes, and other vehicles bring fresh food into the **wholesale** markets. From there, the food is taken to markets or shops, where it is sold to ordinary people.

What caused this food market in Port-au-Prince, Haiti, to be destroyed by **rioters** in 2008?

In 2007, the price of everyday food began to rise steeply. People's wages did not go up at the same speed. With food costing more, and no extra money coming in, people in **developing countries** found it hard to afford even basic food. As a result, there were protests and riots in many cities around the world.

Which of these cities would you rather travel through?

How long will it take these travellers to get to work through the **gridlocked** streets of New Delhi, India? In many cities, lots of people travel in cars. This has led to one of the biggest problems of modern city life: **congestion**.

Congestion happens when there is so much traffic on the roads that it gets jammed up. When congestion is really bad, it can sometimes be quicker to walk than to drive.

Imagine how much faster people will travel on this tram than in the traffic on page 10! Cities like Strasbourg, France, have started to tackle congestion. They have restricted car use in the city centre. Many people use trams, buses, or bicycles.

Congestion-free streets are much clearer and more pleasant. People who live and work in the city can get around more quickly and safely than in the past. Tourists and visitors enjoy the city more.

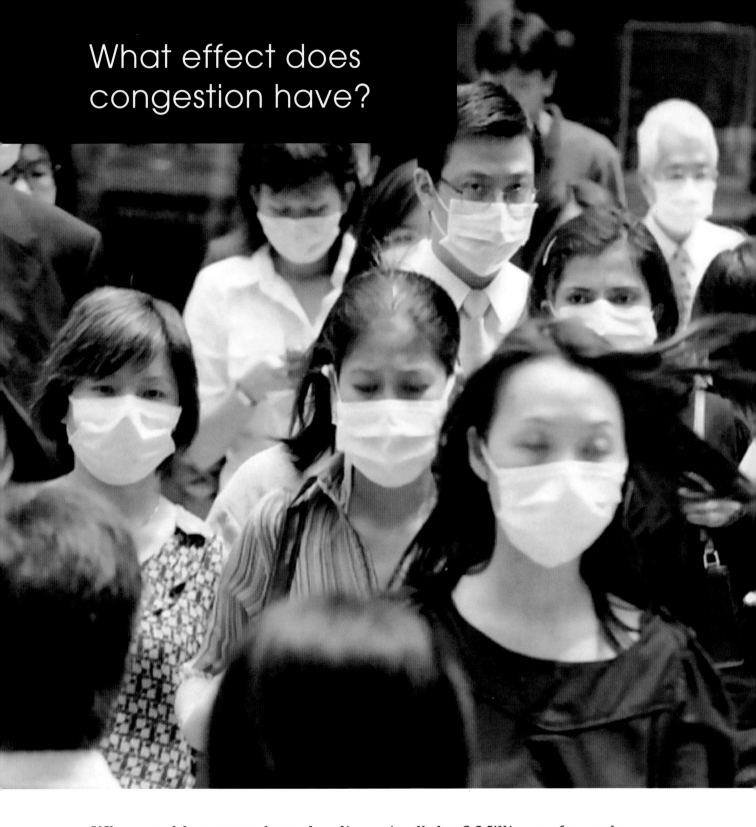

Who would want to breathe dirty air all day? Millions of people living in cities have no choice. Every car, bus, and lorry in a traffic jam is burning fuel, which causes **pollution**. These people in Hong Kong, China, are wearing face masks to try to avoid the fumes.

Pollution from burning **fossil fuels**, including petrol, is one of the main causes of **global warming**. In many places, global warming is causing terrible problems for the **environment** and society.

Some cities have tried to cut pollution from vehicles. In London, the **mayor** introduced a "**congestion**-charging zone" (shown by the "C" on this street sign). Most vehicles were charged to enter the middle of London. Only "cleaner" cars were allowed to travel for free.

Would you want to pay every time you drove into a city? When London's mayor tried to make the zone bigger, it was very unpopular. He was voted out of power at the next election.

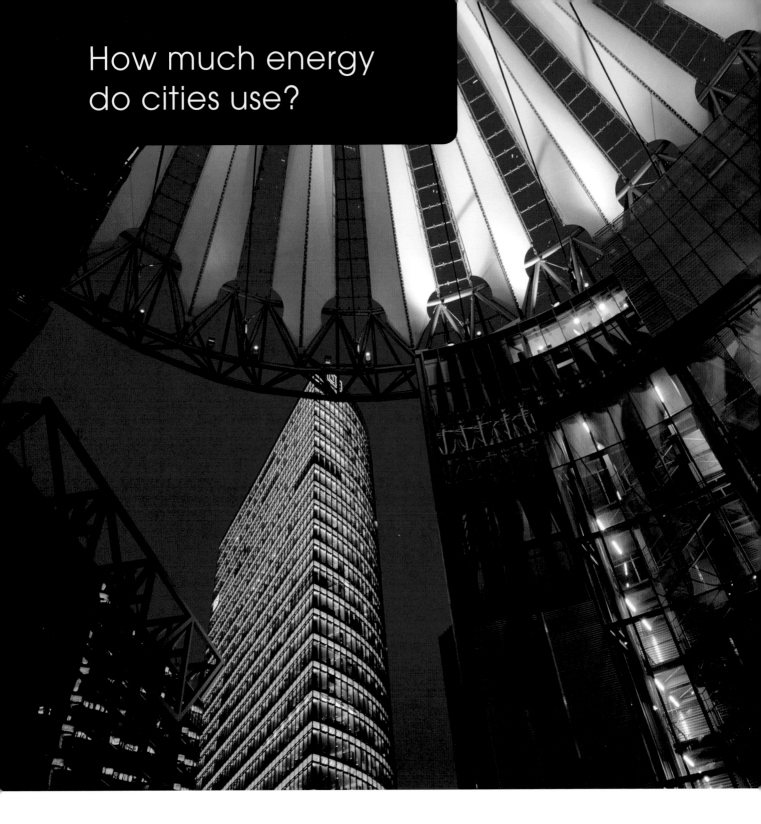

How much energy do cities use?

Do your parents ever tell you to turn off lights to save energy? Perhaps someone should tell whoever owns this building in Berlin, Germany, the same thing. Imagine how much energy is being used to light buildings around the world, even when no one is in them.

Cities use a lot of energy. Most of the energy comes from burning **fossil fuels**. This produces **greenhouse gases**, one of the main causes of **global warming**.

This is Council House 2 in Melbourne, Australia. The building was designed to be **environmentally** friendly. For example, instead of using air conditioning, yellow solar-powered **turbines** draw cool air up through the building at night.

Council House 2 uses only 15 per cent of the electricity and 13 per cent of the gas as the building it replaced. In total, it produces only 13 per cent as much greenhouse gas as the old building.

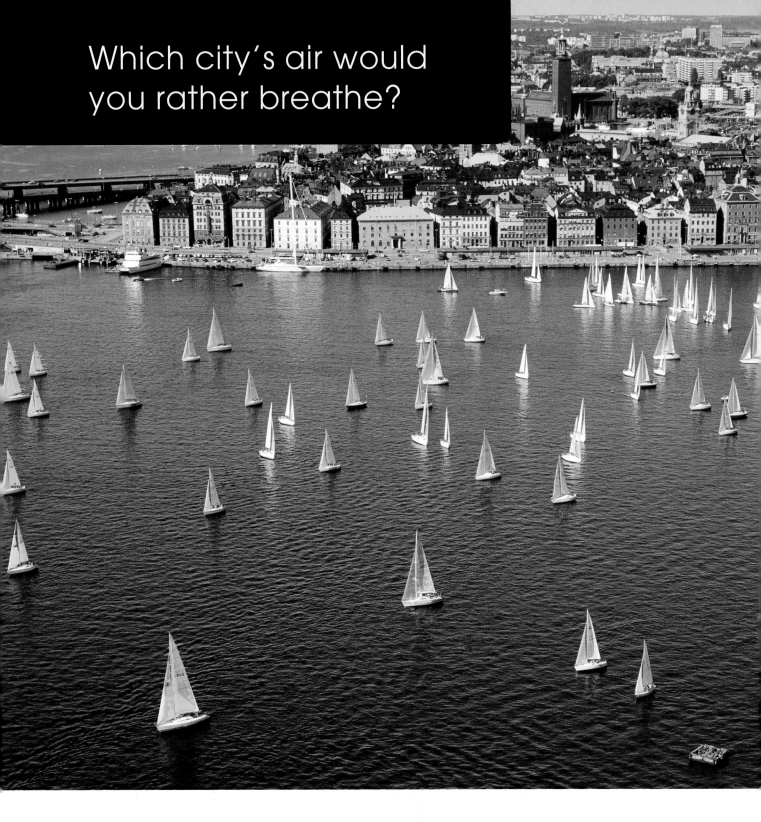

Which city's air would you rather breathe?

Do you think the people of Stockholm, Sweden, ever need to wear face masks like the people from Hong Kong on page 12? Probably not – the factories that once poured **pollution** into Stockholm's **atmosphere** have mostly closed down.

Today, few cities in wealthy countries still have big **industrial** plants. Their industries have moved to cities in countries such as India. They are polluting the air there instead.

What would it be like trying to race through air like this? Before the 2008 Olympics in Beijing, China, many athletes were worried that air pollution would affect them. Sometimes Beijing's pollution is so thick, it is impossible to see more than a few hundred metres ahead. For the Olympics, Beijing's factories were closed down and half the city's cars were banned to try to clear the air. Luckily, most people felt that pollution had not affected the Games. This did not solve Beijing's air problem permanently, though.

Which river would you rather swim in?

This is the Yarra River in Melbourne, Australia. In many older cities like Melbourne, the rivers have been cleaned up. Old **industrial pollution** has been removed. Factories and **sewage** outlets are controlled to make sure they do not pollute the water.

Some city rivers now have fish living in them again for the first time in years. Insect life, river birds, and plants have all come back.

Can you imagine wading through this river in China? The water is so polluted that all the fish have died.

In **developing countries**, pollution is not always well controlled. Factories spill waste into the rivers, poisoning the fish and other river life. People throw their rubbish into the river, where it rots. At the same time, poor people use the rivers for washing and drinking water. The dirty water spreads sickness and disease.

Where does all the sewage go?

These floating homes are in Cambodia. Several hundred people live here. As there are few people, the water can cope with their **sewage**. The sewage is broken up in the water. Sunlight and **bacteria** break down harmful waste. Tiny water creatures eat the good parts.

Many cities began as small villages beside a river. At first, the river could cope with their waste. As the villages grew into cities, the rivers could no longer cope. They became dirty and unhealthy.

Would you want to wash in water from this city stream? It is in Freetown, Sierra Leone. It is **polluted** with sewage.

Rivers cannot cope with large amounts of sewage. When small settlements grow, they need **sewers** to remove the waste instead. But poorer settlements sometimes cannot afford to build sewers. The waste still goes into the river. The dirty water spreads deadly diseases.

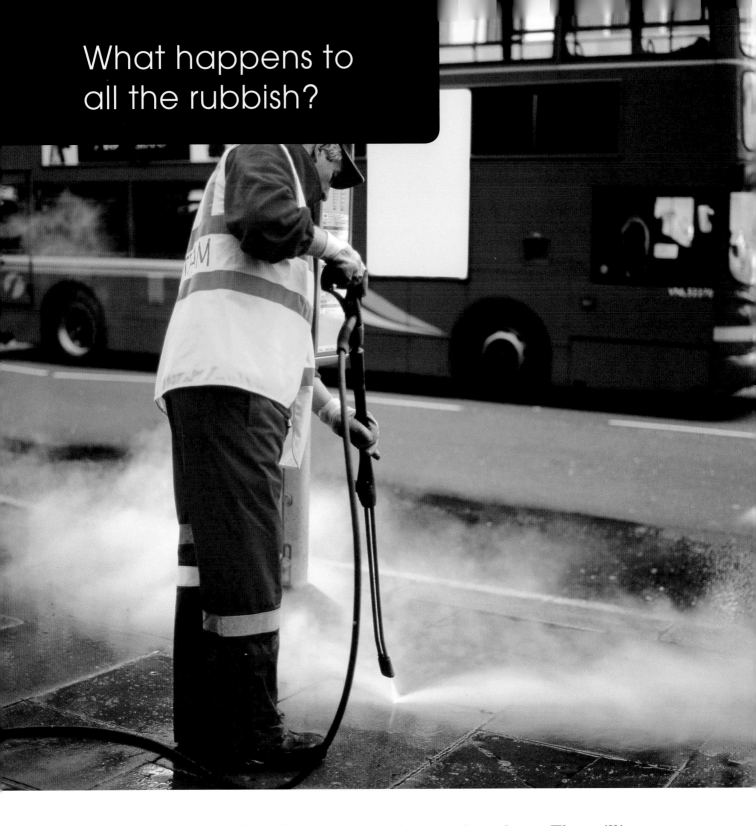

What happens to all the rubbish?

The pavements in London get an early-morning clean. The millions of people who live in cities produce millions of tonnes of waste each year. In many cities the waste is collected by binmen and taken to a local tip. This keeps the streets clean and tidy.

What to do with all our waste is becoming a problem. Much of it used to be buried as **landfill**. However, many landfill sites are now full.

How would you like to step outside in the morning and be greeted by these big piles of rubbish? This photograph of Naples, Italy, shows what can happen if rubbish is not collected.

In the 1990s, Naples began to have difficulty finding anywhere to put its waste. Rubbish was not collected, and began to pile up in the streets. In places, it towered over people's heads. The rat population exploded, and the city stank of rotting food.

Imagine how loud it is standing in the middle of Times Square in New York, USA. Cities can be very noisy places. Traffic, deliveries, shops opening and closing, and building work all add to the din.

People make a lot of noise, too, talking, watching television, and listening to music. When the noise gets too loud, it is called noise pollution. Noise pollution makes life miserable for people, and drives away some wildlife.

In many cities, the authorities are very strict about noise pollution. In some Swiss cities like Zurich, shown here, there are rules about how late you can turn on your washing machine, in case it disturbs your neighbour. Even flushing the toilet at the wrong time of night is discouraged!

Many cities have noise-complaint units. Members of the unit prevent everything from noisy building work to loud parties.

How can we help cities?

What would it be like to have a bike parked on every street corner, ready to use? You probably wouldn't travel by car as often, so there would be less **pollution**.

This cycle scheme in Paris, France, aims to put a bike within easy reach of everyone in the city. For a small amount of money, people can pick up a bike and cycle anywhere in Paris. They then leave the bike in another storage area.

Recycling is one of the ways people can save their cities from being buried under a mountain of waste. Recycling means that less waste has to be buried or burned.

Recycling helps the **environment**, because making goods from recycled material uses less energy and **resources** than making goods from scratch. Even better is to re-use goods, such as shopping bags, instead of taking a new one each time.

WHAT DID YOU FIND OUT ABOUT CITIES?

How do cities affect the rest of the world?
Hint: try making a list of the things cities get from other countries. The photographs on pages 8, 14, and 18 might give you some starting points.

Are all cities the same? Can you think of some differences?
Tip: the photographs all through the book will help you to decide your answer, but pages 4, 7, 10, 16, and 21 might be especially useful.

What makes a city a good place to live?
Hint: try making a list of all the good things about city life. The photographs on pages 6, 8, 16, and 25 might give you some ideas, but you will probably be able to think of other things too.

What makes some cities unpleasant places to live?
Tip: there are photographs of some of the unpleasant things about living in some cities on pages 7, 9, 10, 12, 17, 19, 21, and 23. Do any of these look like a city you know?

What is the best way to travel around a city?
Hint: make a list of all the ways of travelling around a city, then give each type of transport a mark out of 10 for speed, comfort, and effect on the **environment**. The photographs on pages 10–11, 12, 22, and 26 should give you some ideas.

Why are some cities raising a stink – and what should we do about it?
Tip: have a look at the picture on page 23. Can you think of ways to make sure this does not happen in a city that you visit?

Where do cities get their energy from? Could they use less of it?
Hint: start by looking at the photographs on pages 10–11 and 14–15. How many different types of energy can you list? Do you think all this energy use is necessary? Could some of it be reduced, or cut back altogether?

What would life be like without cities?
Tip: think about where people's food would come from. Also, where would everyone live? Could everyone have electricity and water if we didn't all live so close together?

How could some cities be improved?
Hint: use your answers to the other questions for this one. What things could be changed in a city you visit that would make life better for the people who live there? Are there things the city's people could do to help the environment, both in the city and outside it?

Glossary

atmosphere layer of gases surrounding Earth, including the group of gases we call air. Without a healthy atmosphere, life on Earth would become impossible.

bacteria one of the smallest types of living creature. Even though they are so tiny, bacteria do lots of useful jobs, such as eating waste products.

congestion queues of traffic caused by too many vehicles being on the road

developing country usually a country that is poor but becoming wealthier. Developing countries are often becoming more industrial, rather than relying on farming, and their cities often grow rapidly.

dweller person living in a certain place

environment landscape, soil, weather, plants, and animals that together make one place different from another

facility thing or place that has a special purpose

fossil fuel coal, petroleum oil, and gas. Fossil fuels can be burnt to produce energy. When they are burnt they release greenhouse gases, one of the causes of global warming.

global warming rise in Earth's average temperature

greenhouse gas gas that traps heat within Earth's atmosphere. If too many greenhouse gases build up, too much heat gets trapped and the temperature rises. This is called global warming.

gridlock standstill because there are too many vehicles on the road and none of them can move

illegal against the law

industrial businesses and activities that produce goods for sale

landfill waste that is buried underground in huge pits, which are then covered with a layer of soil

mayor leader of a city

pollution dirt that harms the environment

recycling using something again to make a new product

resource useful raw material

rioter person taking part in a violent demonstration or protest

rural in or from the countryside

sewage human toilet waste mixed with water

sewer tunnel that carries sewage away to be disposed of safely

turbine set of turning blades which is used to make things happen. They can be used to draw cool air throughout a building.

urban in or from a town or city

wholesale selling large amounts to merchants such as shopkeepers. The merchants will then sell smaller amounts to ordinary people.

Find out more

Books

City Explorer, Neil Morris (Raintree, 2004)

Clean Planet: Stopping Litter and Pollution, Tristan Boyer Binns
(Heinemann Library, 2005)

Global Cities, various (Evans Brothers, 2006 and 2007)

Who Eats Who in City Habitats?, Robert Snedden (Franklin Watts, 2005)

Websites

www.un.org/cyberschoolbus/habitat

A United Nations website, specially designed for young people. It includes
information about cities, an imagined perfect city, information on dealing
with city life, and much more.

www.greenpeace.org.uk/climate

This section of the **environmental** charity Greenpeace's website is about
climate change, its causes, and its effects. It includes a useful section on
things you can do to help stop **global warming**.

Index